BEES, BUGS & BUTTERFLIES

BEES, BUGS & BUTTERFLIES

JUDITH SIMONS

PHOTOGRAPHS BY GLORIA NICOL

LORENZ BOOKS

LONDON • NEW YORK • SYDNEY • BATH

First published in 1996 by Lorenz Books

© 1996 Anness Publishing Limited

Lorenz Books is an imprint of
Anness Publishing Limited
1 Boundary Row
London SE1 8HP

This edition is distributed in Canada by
Raincoast Books Distribution Limited

ISBN 1 85967 282 5

Publisher: Joanna Lorenz
Project Editor: Judith Simons
Copy Editor: Beverley Jollands
Designer: Michael R. Carter
Photographer: Gloria Nicol
Step Photographer: Lucy Tizard
Illustrator: Lucinda Ganderton

Printed in Singapore by Star Standard Industries Pte Ltd.

Contents

INTRODUCTION

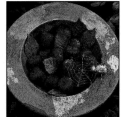

It's been estimated that there are at least five million species of insects, of which only about one million have so far actually been identified. This astonishingly large family of mini-beasts comes in a huge variety of forms, colours and sizes. With their strange eyes, numerous legs, stings and bites, they are a source of horrified fascination to us. They seem to arrive on a warm day as if from nowhere, or transform themselves beyond recognition: wriggling caterpillars become iridescent butterflies, fat blue larvae turn into enamelled ladybirds. Their shapes and colours defy our wildest imagination, so it's not surprising that they have taken their place as motifs in art and design, as both inspiration and symbol.

An early and outstanding example of their symbolic status is the scarab beetle, revered by the ancient Egyptians as the symbol of resurrection. They compared it with their sun-god who was credited with creating himself, as the beetle appeared to do. Beautiful gold winged scarabs inlaid with cloisonné work and semi-precious stones were the central motifs of bracelets, rings and necklaces which adorned the mummies of the dead pharaohs.

Above: Typical of the period, this beautiful Dutch flower painting is alive with insects; Ambrosius Bosschaert the Elder, 1614.

Butterflies assumed a similar role, as the butterfly emerging from its chrysalis represented the soul leaving the body. Dutch emblem books of the sixteenth century contained closely observed miniature paintings of butterflies and many other animals and plants that carried complicated symbolic meanings for the noble patrons who commissioned the books. Their detail was so intricate that naturalists are easily able to identify the species these miniaturists painted. This precision evolved into the magnificent Dutch flower paintings of the seventeenth century, which continued to crawl with lifelike butterflies, beetles and bugs.

The natural association of insects with flowers has meant that they inevitably appear as details in floral designs, particularly when the patterns are naturalistic and free-flowing, such as the richly embroidered silks produced in Lyons in the eighteenth century. The earliest known piece of English soft-paste porcelain, made at the Chelsea factory in 1745, is known as the Goat and Bee jug. In addition to two goats it features a twig-shaped handle and a moulded bee sitting on flowers.

In Florence a form of mosaic called *pietra dura* was used for tabletops and on a much smaller scale in jewellery. A marble ground was inlaid with many different coloured marbles as well as semi-precious stones such as coral and lapis lazuli. Birds, insects and flowers were popular themes in this spectacular craft. Insects as decorative motifs became less evident in the restrained designs of neo-classicism, although Empire-style decorations commissioned by Napoleon featured his personal emblem, the bee, on

Above: Goat and Bee Jug; Chelsea, 1745.

ormolu mounts and brocade chair covers.

It has to be said that artists and craftsmen have always been selective in the insects they have chosen to decorate their work. Everyone loves a ladybird or a butterfly, but we don't feel so warmly towards dung beetles or large furry moths. Bees score highly, wasps do not. Flies are distinctly unpopular, although mummified in amber they become extremely desirable.

In the 1860s insect jewellery was the vogue. Even cockroaches made an appearance. Hat pins were decorated with carved ivory or enamelled butterflies. Men's tie pins were topped with flies, bees, wasps and butterflies in diamonds with ruby or sapphire eyes. By the 1870s they were even using real insects: South American beetles with very hard wing

Below: A minutely observed Dutch engraving; 1705.

Above: Florentine pietra dura *tabletop.*

Right: Precious gem and enamel jewellery; c 1890.

demand for their lovely turquoise wings to be mounted in silver jewellery. The Fabergé workshops included insects in their repertoire of precious Easter eggs, creating a miniature egg in the form of a ladybird which was designed to be worn as a pendant.

In Victorian homes, gentlemen pulled off their boots with the help of cast-iron stag-beetle boot-jacks, wedging their heels between the insect's antennae. The black armour-plating and outlandish size of the real insects suits them very well to this design. Iron flies with hinged wings stood by the kitchen range to hold the matches, and similar boxes were made of glass and silver for the dining table.

cases in metallic greenish-blue were set in gold or silver. More recently, Brazilian blue butterflies have been decimated satisfying the

Butterflies were a prominent motif of Art Nouveau. The swirling designs of their wings suited its curving, organic forms. They were prevalent in Japanese art (in which they again symbolized the soul) and this had a significant influence on *fin-de-siècle* artists and architects when prints from Japan began to be widely circulated in Europe. James McNeill Whistler signed his paintings with a butterfly. In New York, the Tiffany company produced Art Nouveau-style lamps and vases in coloured and iridescent glass decorated with butterflies and dragonflies.

Until the arrival of photography, insect discoveries were documented in the meticulous engravings which illustrated natural history books and in elaborate collections of the insects themselves, pinned and labelled in taxonomic order. Though these arrangements now seem macabre, they may inspire you to echo their orderly designs in paint or needlework. Engravings can be a wonderful design source. Their clear black-and-white images are particularly appropriate to insects such as beetles, and these days you can easily employ them in your own designs by using a photocopier imaginatively.

As many insects resemble works of art themselves, they'll suggest plenty of ideas for ways to use them in your own designs. The bright shiny colours of beetles and ladybirds make them good decorations for glossily-painted furniture and toys: children find friendly ladybirds especially appealing. Butterflies, dragonflies and silvery moths are better suited to transparent, iridescent fabrics or embroidery. While spiders aren't actually insects, the ethereal beauty and natural geometry of their webs makes it impossible to exclude their contribution to the lovely design ideas in this book. Try some of these projects, or use them as inspiration for original creations of your own, and take a fresh look at creepy-crawlies and their fascinating world.

Top left: Pâte-de-verre *bowls; Gabriel Argy-Rousseau.*

Left: "Georgette", an opalescent glass bonbonnière; Lalique.

BEETLE STATIONERY

Hunt through nineteenth-century natural history books for engravings of weird and wonderful beetles, which you can use to decorate a matching set of greetings cards, envelopes, gift tags and postcards.

YOU WILL NEED

MATERIALS
*thin card and writing paper
  in various colours and white
ready-made envelopes
photocopies of beetles
matt gold paper
glue-stick
gold cord*

EQUIPMENT
*craft knife
ruler
cutting mat
scissors
hole punch*

1 For postcards, use a craft knife and ruler to cut the coloured card to a suitable size. Measure your envelopes and cut the greetings cards to fit neatly inside when folded. Score down the centre with the blunt edge of the scissors. Use the offcuts for gift tags, punching a single hole in the top.

2 Cut round the beetle motifs with the craft knife and ruler, making neat rectangles. Tear squares and rectangles of various sizes from the coloured card and gold paper.

3 Arrange the beetle shapes in a pleasing design on the paper or card. Stick each piece down with a glue-stick. Make sure the glue reaches right to the edges so that they don't curl up. Stick single motifs on the flaps of the envelopes and at the top of the writing paper. To complete the tags, thread a length of gold cord through each hole.

CHILD'S LADYBIRD CHAIR

Ladybirds are always welcome in their paintbox-bright uniforms. Add fun and interest to an ordinary white chair by getting a procession of the little creatures to meander across it. This simple decoration will make it any child's favourite seat.

YOU WILL NEED

MATERIALS
child's chair
acrylic paint: red and black
acrylic varnish: oak and clear

EQUIPMENT
card or paper
pencil
fine paintbrush
decorator's paintbrush
cloth

1 Make a simple template in the shape of a ladybird's head and body from card or paper. Draw round it with a pencil, making the ladybirds trail up and across the chair.

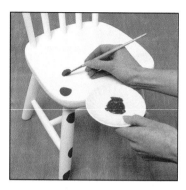

2 Using a fine paintbrush, fill in the bodies of the ladybirds with red paint. Leave to dry.

3 Draw round the ladybirds and add the heads, legs and spots using black paint and a fine paintbrush. Leave to dry.

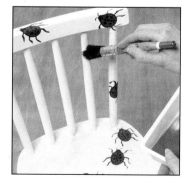

4 Thin the oak varnish with water and paint on using a decorator's paintbrush. Rub off immediately with a clean cloth. Apply a coat of clear varnish.

SPIDER'S WEB BROOCH

Reproduce the delicate texture of a web in glittering copper and silver wire. The resident spider is resplendent in blue and gold and not at all threatening, especially as she has only six legs and a curly tail!

YOU WILL NEED

MATERIALS
1 mm/0.039 in copper wire
0.65 mm/0.024 in silver wire
self-hardening modelling
  clay
two small glass beads
strong glue
brooch pin
turquoise acrylic paint
clear varnish
gold powder

EQUIPMENT
wire cutters
round-nosed jewellery pliers
modelling tool
paintbrush

1 Cut four 8 cm/3 in lengths of copper wire. Curl both ends of each piece into a loop with the pliers.

2 Arrange the pieces to form a star. Wrap the silver wire round the centre. Working outwards in a spiral, twist the silver wire once round each copper wire. Secure and trim.

3 Cut six 6 cm/2½ in lengths of copper wire. Curl one end of each into a loop then bend into the shape of the spider's legs.

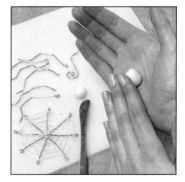

4 Cut an 8 cm/3 in length of wire and bend into a spiral for the tail. Roll two balls of clay for the body and head.

►

5 Press the two clay balls together, joining securely with the help of the modelling tool. Smooth the surface of the clay with wet fingers or the modelling tool.

6 Insert the looped ends of the wire legs and tail into the spider's body. Press two glass beads into the head to make the eyes.

7 Press the spider's body on to the wire web. Flatten a small piece of clay and attach it to the spider from underneath the web, using the modelling tool to join it securely. Leave the clay to harden.

8 Glue the brooch pin to the back of the spider, and secure the legs and tail with drops of glue. Paint the body and head turquoise and leave to dry. Apply a coat of varnish to seal the paint. Mix gold powder with a little varnish and apply swiftly with a dry brush to leave some of the turquoise paint showing through.

NEEDLEPOINT BEETLE

This delightful beetle on his subtly coloured background is easy to work in tent stitch. Measure the frame you have chosen and work enough of the background to ensure that no bare canvas will be visible when the picture is framed.

YOU WILL NEED

MATERIALS
25 cm/10 in square needlepoint canvas with 24 holes per 5 cm/12 holes per in picture frame
tapestry yarns as listed in the chart key at the back of the book

EQUIPMENT
waterproof marker pen
masking tape
scissors
tapestry needle
iron
pressing cloth
dressmaker's pins

1 Prepare the canvas. Mark a vertical line down the centre and a horizontal line across the centre using a waterproof pen. Mark the edges of the aperture in the frame you intend to use, positioning it centrally over the marked lines.

2 Bind the edges of the canvas with masking tape to keep it straight and prevent the yarn catching as you sew.

3 Cut a 45 cm/18 in length of tapestry wool and work the design from the chart at the back of the book in tent stitch. Start from the centre and work outwards to help keep the piece from distorting as you sew. When the design is completed and the background is large enough to fill the frame, remove the masking tape.

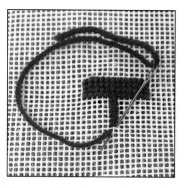

4 Use a hot iron and a damp cloth to steam the work gently, pulling it into shape as you go. If the canvas is very distorted, pin it into shape on the ironing board before steaming it. Dry the canvas thoroughly and quickly.

TENT STITCH Begin with a knot on the right side of the canvas, bringing the needle up again about 2.5 cm/1 in away. Work the first few stitches over this thread to secure it; the knot can then be cut away neatly. To work tent stitch, insert the needle one row up and one row to the right, bringing it back up through the hole to the left of your starting-point. All the stitches must slant in the same direction – at the end of a row turn the canvas upside down to work the next row.

VERTICAL TENT STITCH Tent stitch is worked horizontally, but it can be worked vertically where necessary. Always keep the stitches on the reverse side longer and more sloping than those on the front to avoid distorting the fabric. Try to keep an even tension and do not pull too tightly.

5 Cut away the excess canvas and mount your picture into the frame.

T I N   C A N   I N S E C T S

There's more than one way to recycle empty cans: these lighthearted designs turn them into insects to crawl up your garden walls. Use beer or lager cans that have the same logos on the front and back so that your insects will look symmetrical. The bar code makes a stripy body. Take care not to cut yourself on the sharp edges.

YOU WILL NEED

MATERIALS
*large steel drinks can, top and
 bottom removed*

EQUIPMENT
*strong scissors with small points
adhesive tape
large paintbrush with a tapered
 handle
small long-nosed pliers*

1 Trace the template from the back of the book. Cut up the side of the can opposite the bar code and open out flat. Place the template in position and secure with adhesive tape. Cut round the template carefully with sharp scissors.

2 Place the body of the insect over the tapered handle of a paintbrush, with the fattest part nearest the head. Shape the body by bending it round the handle. Fold the lower wings very slightly under the body and bend the upper wings forward, folding them slightly over the top part of the body.

3 Using long-nosed pliers, twist the antennae back on themselves and curl the ends.

DRAGONFLY-PRINT BOX

The background of this bold dragonfly print has been roughly cut to give it the look of a primitive woodcut. If you haven't tried lino-cutting before, practise on an offcut. Make sure the tools are very sharp and always keep your free hand out of the way of the cutting edge. Don't dig too deep.

YOU WILL NEED

MATERIALS
thick yellow paper
water-based block printing
 paints: red, green and black
lino tile
PVA glue
wooden box
clear varnish

EQUIPMENT
tracing paper
pencil
carbon paper
paintbrush
lino cutters
craft knife
glass sheet
lino roller
small decorator's paintbrush

1 Trace the outlines of the dragonfly motifs from the back of the book, adapting the size as necessary. Using carbon paper, transfer on to the paper and paint in red and green. Trace the completed dragonfly motifs, turn the tracing over and transfer on to the lino, giving a reverse image.

2 Cut out the design on the lino, cutting a criss-cross pattern freehand on the wings to give a lacy effect. Cut out the background roughly, leaving some areas untouched to give texture to the design. Trim the lino round the design to make positioning easier.

3 Spread the black paint on the glass sheet with the roller and roll it evenly on to the lino cut. Position the lino cut carefully on the paper and apply even pressure to make the print. Leave the print to dry, then glue it to the top of the box. Seal and protect it with a coat of varnish.

SALT AND PEPPER BUGS

A request to pass the salt will be the starting signal for these eager mobile ladybirds to wheel their way down the table to you. They're based on toy trucks with a friction drive, and are sure to be a big hit at family mealtimes.

YOU WILL NEED

MATERIALS
pair of matching toy trucks
matching salt and pepper
 pots
polymer clay: black, red and
 white
coloured paperclips
epoxy resin glue
clear gloss varnish
enamel paints: red and black

EQUIPMENT
screwdriver
stiff card for template
pencil
scissors
rolling pin
craft knife
pliers
paintbrush

1 Undo the fixing screws and remove the body from each toy truck.

2 Mark out two matching templates which will fit over the truck chassis and round the bases of the salt and pepper pots, leaving a rim of approximately 5 mm/^{1}/$_2$ in. Cut out of stiff card.

3 Roll a piece of black clay thinly to cover the template. Cut to shape. Stand the salt cellar in position on the base and mould a sausage of clay round it.

4 Press a ball of clay on to the front of the template and mould into shape for the head of the ladybird. Make two holes for the feelers with the end of a paperclip. Remove the pot and template carefully. Make a matching base for the pepper pot in the same way.

5 Straighten out the paperclips and trim to length for the feelers. Roll four small balls of red clay and make a hole in each with a paperclip. Mould two pairs of eyes from white and black clay.

6 Roll a ball of red clay for each truck wheel and press it on, moulding it into a dome shape. Remove carefully.

7 Bake all the clay elements in a low oven according to the manufacturer's instructions. Fix everything in place with epoxy resin glue, avoiding the drive mechanism in the truck chassis. Varnish the wheel hubs.

8 Paint the salt and pepper pots in bright red. Allow to dry, then add ladybird spots in black. Allow to dry.

CREEPY-CRAWLY HANDKERCHIEF

A handkerchief full of bugs sounds alarming, but these little prints adapted from nineteenth-century folk-art woodcuts are anything but. If the handkerchief has a self-weave pattern you can use this as a guide to placing the prints; if not, scatter them randomly but make sure they are evenly spaced over the fabric. Practise making the prints on a spare piece of fabric.

YOU WILL NEED

MATERIALS
15 cm/6 in square lino tile
fabric paints, in various colours
fabric paint medium
new white handkerchief,
 laundered to remove dressing

EQUIPMENT
craft knife
tracing paper
pencil
lino cutters
paintbrush

1 Cut the lino into six pieces about 5 x 7.5 cm/2 x 3 in. Trace the motifs at the back of the book and transfer them to the lino.

2 Use a V-shaped lino tool to cut round the outlines of the bugs. Use a wider tool to cut away the rest of the background.

3 Apply fabric paint to the blocks. Using a paintbrush, you can blend the colours to achieve interesting effects. Dilute the paint as necessary with fabric medium.

4 Place the block on the fabric, press evenly over the back and lift it up carefully to avoid smudging the print. Follow the paint manufacturer's instructions to fix the colours.

DANCING BEES BOX

The bees encircling this painted box have been cut out of folded paper like a row of dancing dolls. Measure the lid before you begin and enlarge or reduce the template so that the ring of bees will fit well. This box would make a wonderful gift filled with pots of honey or beeswax cosmetics.

YOU WILL NEED

MATERIALS
circular painted box
black paper
yellow acrylic paint
all-purpose glue
clear varnish

EQUIPMENT
white marker pencil
scissors
paintbrush
small decorator's paintbrush

1 Trace the template from the back of the book and adjust the size to fit your box as necessary. Fold a sheet of black paper in half, then in half again. Position the template across the folded corner so that the tips of the wings are touching the folds, and draw round it with the white pencil.

2 Cut out, making sure that the bees are joined by their wings. Unfold the bees carefully. Make two sets. Draw the bees' stripes on each circle and paint their stripes and wings in yellow acrylic paint.

3 Glue the bees to the lid of the box. Cut the second set in half and stick them on the sides of the box. Protect the box with a coat of varnish.

SPIDER'S WEB CLOCK

Buy gold-coloured hands for your clock, which will match the gilded spider and contrast prettily with the rich blue background.

YOU WILL NEED

MATERIALS
6 mm/¹/₄ in birch plywood, approximately 18 cm/7 in square
white undercoat paint
acrylic paint: dark blue, white, black and gold
clear matt varnish
clock movement and hands

EQUIPMENT
pair of compasses
pencil
ruler
drill
fret saw or coping saw
sandpaper
paintbrushes: medium, stiff and fine
white marker pencil

1 Draw a circle on the plywood and divide into eight segments using a ruler. Draw the looping outline of the web round the edge.

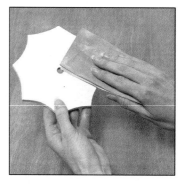

2 Drill a hole in the centre and saw round the edge of the web. Sand, then paint with white undercoat. Leave to dry and sand again.

3 Paint the clock face in dark blue and stipple with a stiff brush while the paint is still wet. Apply a coat of matt varnish. When dry, draw the web pattern with a white marker pencil.

4 Paint over the web using light grey acrylic and a fine brush. Paint on the flies and the golden spider. Finish with a coat of matt varnish and attach the clock movement and hands.

SILVER MOTH SCARF

Ethereal silvery moths flutter delicately over one side of this lovely silk scarf, their glitter reflected in the pleated organza on the other side. Check your sewing machine manual for details of how to do free machine embroidery.

YOU WILL NEED

MATERIALS
fusible bonding web
small amounts of contrasting silk, velvet and organza
142 x 30 cm/56 x 12 in silk satin
matching fine machine embroidery thread
142 x 30 cm/56 x 12 in pleated metallic organza
matching sewing thread

EQUIPMENT
pencil
iron
scissors
embroidery hoop
sewing machine
dressmaker's pins
sewing needle

1 Trace the templates from the back of the book. Lay the fusible bonding web over the templates and trace as many moths as you need. Press the bonding to the wrong side of the contrasting silk. Trace the same number of body shapes on the bonding and press to the wrong side of the velvet. Cut out all the shapes. Remove the backing paper and press all the shapes to the right side of the silk satin.

2 Place the satin in an embroidery hoop. Cut some pieces of organza slightly larger than the moths and machine-stitch them to the satin following the outlines of the wings. Trim the organza carefully close to the line of stitching round each motif.

3 Work two or three lines of stitching round each moth to conceal the raw edges. Pin the pleated organza to the satin with right sides together, and stitch all round the edge leaving a gap of 10 cm/4 in in one side. Turn the scarf to the right side and slip-stitch the gap.

I N S E C T   S T O R A G E   B O X

If you have access to a photocopier you can make up striking and original designs on paper. Flies, beetles and spiders all look very effective in black and white. Before you begin to print your paper for this project, it's a good idea to measure your box carefully and keep a note of all the dimensions to be sure that your design will fit well.

YOU WILL NEED

MATERIALS
insect images
white A3 paper
glue-stick
shoe box
white acrylic or poster paint
PVA glue
black paper
clear matt varnish

EQUIPMENT
ruler
photocopier
scissors
paintbrush

1 Photocopy the insect images to the desired size. Arrange the insects on A3 paper and secure in place with the glue-stick. When you are happy with your arrangement, make enough copies of it to cover the box, plus a few spares in case you go wrong. Two designs have been used here: one with a large central motif for the top of the box, and the other with insects scattered all over the paper.

2 If the box is printed, give it a coat of white paint and allow to dry. Brush a thin layer of PVA glue over the top and sides of the lid. Position your covering paper carefully and smooth out from the centre to exclude air bubbles. Make a straight cut to each corner of the lid top and trim the overlap at the corners and edges to 2 cm/³/₄ in. Carefully smooth the paper down over the sides, glueing each flap under the next side piece to make neat corners, and tucking the overlap inside the lid.

3 Measure the sides of the box, adding 2 cm/³/₄ in to each dimension, and cut four pieces of paper. Glue and cover the inner sides.

4 From the paper you used for the lid, cut the lining for the bottom to the exact size of the box and glue in place.

5 Cut a rectangle from the black paper large enough to cover the bottom and sides of the box and allowing a 2 cm/³/₄ in overlap all round. Cut out a wavy edge 1 cm/¹/₄ in deep. Make straight cuts to the corners of the box and trim the flaps, as before. Glue the paper to the box, turning in the edging.

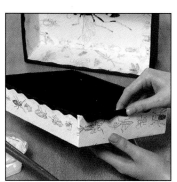

6 Measure the inside of the box lid and cut a piece of black paper to fit, again allowing a 2 cm/³/₄ in overlap. Cut the wavy edge and trim the corners as before. Glue in place.

7 Dilute some PVA glue with water and brush all over the box and lid. This will go on cloudy but will clear as it dries. Finally seal the box with a coat of acrylic varnish.

BUSY BEE WORKBOX

You'll find any number of uses for this handy box. The stylized fretwork bee – the symbol of industry – is both decorative and functional, as it forms the handle of the box.

YOU WILL NEED

MATERIALS
9 mm/³/₈ in pine slat, 2 m x
7 cm/6 ft 6 in x 2³/₄ in
wood glue
4 mm/³/₁₆ in birch plywood,
38 x 20 cm/15 x 8 in
panel pins (optional)
light oak wood stain
polyurethane varnish
38 x 19 cm/15 x 7¹/₂ in
self-adhesive baize

EQUIPMENT
tenon saw
pencil
carbon paper
6 mm/¹/₄ in drill
fret saw
sandpaper
hammer (optional)
paintbrush
fine wire wool
scissors

1 Cut two 38 cm/15 in lengths of pine. Glue the two pieces together to form a single piece.

2 Trace the bee motif from the back of the book and transfer to the centre of the board using carbon paper.

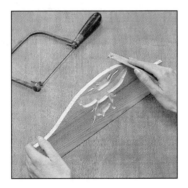

3 Drill a hole through each section of the bee. Pass the saw blade through each hole and saw out the design. Mark and saw the curve of the handle, making the ends 6.5 cm/2¹/₂ in deep. Sand smooth.

4 Cut two 39.8 cm/15³/₄ in and two 20 cm/8 in lengths of pine for the sides of the box. Glue these round the plywood base. You may find it easier to fix the corners with panel pins while the glue dries.

5 Glue the handle section into place. Colour the box with wood stain and allow to dry, then varnish it.

6 Rub down the workbox with fine wire wool to achieve a warm lustre. Cut the baize in half and trim to fit into the base of the box.

GRASSHOPPER-ON-A-STICK

P lant this bold, bright grasshopper in your garden or conservatory and let him add a splash of colour among the foliage.

YOU WILL NEED

MATERIALS
9 mm/³/₈ in pine slat, 5.5 x
  23 cm/2¹/₄ x 9 in
two pieces of 6 mm/¹/₄ in
  birch plywood each 10 x
  24 cm/4 x 9¹/₂ in
wood glue
6 mm/¹/₄ in dowel, 48 cm/
  19 in long
white undercoat paint
enamel paints, in various
  colours

EQUIPMENT
pencil
fret saw
double-sided tape
craft knife
sandpaper
6 mm/¹/₄ in drill
medium and fine
  paintbrushes
empty wine bottle

1 Trace the templates from the back of the book. Draw the body on the pine slat and cut out. Stick the two pieces of plywood together with double-sided tape and cut out the legs, sawing through both pieces at once. Cut out the antennae from plywood. Use a craft knife to whittle the edges of the body and sand down to give a rounded shape. Sand the rough edges of all the pieces.

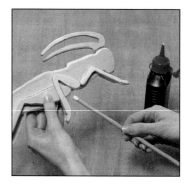

2 Drill a hole in the underside of the body. Glue the legs and antennae in position on the body and stick the dowel in the hole.

3 Paint with white undercoat and leave to dry standing in an empty wine bottle. Colour the grasshopper with enamel paints.

SGRAFFITO EGG

The familiar scraper-board technique takes on a new delicacy when applied to the fragile surface of a real eggshell. Try to find an egg with a pale shell. To blow it, carefully make a small hole in the pointed end and a larger hole in the round end. Blow through the small hole, holding the egg over a bowl to catch the contents. When working, remember that the egg is very delicate: apply even pressure and don't hold it too tightly.

YOU WILL NEED

MATERIALS
blown egg
acrylic paint: purple-brown
  and dark blue

EQUIPMENT
pencil
paintbrush
craft knife
white marker pencil

1 Draw a cameo outline on the front and back of the shell in pencil. Paint the two oval shapes in purple-brown acrylic, allowing one side to dry before you turn the egg over. You may need two coats. Paint the band round the egg in dark blue, again using two coats if required. Allow to dry thoroughly.

2 Use the point of a craft knife blade to scratch double lines between the brown and blue sections. Make a criss-cross pattern across the blue section and mark a dot in each diamond. Scratch a series of dots between the double lines of the borders.

3 Using a white marker pencil, very lightly sketch the outline of an insect in each brown oval. You can copy the moth in the photograph or use a natural history print as a reference. Engrave the design following the white pencil line, adding more intricate details.

EMBROIDERED DRAGONFLIES

These beautiful iridescent creatures look ready to fly away! If you've never tried free machine embroidery before, look in your sewing machine manual for details.

YOU WILL NEED

MATERIALS
hot or cold water-soluble fabric
opalescent cellophane (or cellophane sweet wrappers)
small pieces of sheer synthetic organza: brown and green
fine metallic thread
thicker metallic thread
spray varnish
glitter pipecleaners
fine wire and a few glass beads for the butterflies

EQUIPMENT
embroidery hoop
felt-tipped pen
dressmaker's pins
sewing machine with fine needle
scissors
kitchen paper
piece of card
sewing needle

1 Stretch the water-soluble fabric on to the embroidery hoop (if it is soluble in cold water, use a double layer). Trace the designs from the back of the book on to the fabric using a felt-tipped pen. Sandwich the cellophane between the two sheer fabrics and pin under the hoop. Machine round the wing details in straight stitch using fine metallic thread.

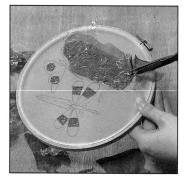

2 Remove the hoop from the machine and trim away the spare fabric and cellophane with scissors.

3 With fine metallic thread in the needle and the thicker metallic thread on the bobbin, machine all round the outlines of the insects in ordinary straight stitch.

4 Put the fine thread on the bobbin and fill in between the outlines, joining all parts of the design. To stiffen the edges, go over the outlines again in zigzag stitch.

5 Check that all the outlines are linked up by holding your work up to the light. Remove from the hoop and dissolve away the fabric in water. Dry on kitchen paper.

6 Pin the insects out flat on a piece of card and spray with varnish. Leave to dry.

7 Cut a piece of glitter pipecleaner longer than the dragonfly body and sew it to the underside of the body part as far as the head.

8 Trim the pipecleaner when you reach the head and bend the rest of the embroidery under the head and upper body to cover the pipecleaner. Stitch in place. Finally, fold the wings together and secure with a few stitches near the body so that the wings are raised.

9 Thread some small glass beads on to fine gold wire and twist into two antennae for the butterfly. Thread these on to the head then complete as for the dragonfly.

BUTTERFLY GIFT-WRAP

Original, hand-printed wrapping paper can make an ordinary present into something very special. Once you've tried stencilling you may never want to buy printed gift-wrap again.

You Will Need

MATERIALS
coloured paper
acrylic paint: red and
  black

EQUIPMENT
acetate sheet
black marker pen
craft knife
cutting mat
masking tape
stiff brush

1 Trace the butterfly template at the back of the book and enlarge it as necessary. Place a piece of acetate over it and use a marker pen to draw the wings for the first stencil. Use a second piece of acetate to make a second stencil of the body and wing markings.

2 Cut out both stencils carefully using a craft knife. Secure the first stencil lightly to the paper with masking tape and stipple on the red paint. Do not overload the brush. Reposition the acetate and repeat to cover the paper.

3 When the red paint is dry, secure the second stencil in place with masking tape. As the acetate is clear it is easy to position the stencil accurately. Stipple on the black paint and repeat to complete the butterflies.

EMBROIDERED INSECT DISPLAY

This design is inspired by Victorian display cases containing rows of beetles and bugs. It's ecologically sound, however, because these stylish black bugs are embroidered on calico.

YOU WILL NEED

MATERIALS
30 cm/12 in square natural calico
stranded embroidery thread: black, ochre, emerald and yellow
20 cm/8 in square thick card
strong button thread
three small labels
pen
square wooden frame to fit a 20 cm/8 in square

EQUIPMENT
thick tracing paper
transfer pencil
iron
embroidery hoop
embroidery needle
large sewing needle

1 Enlarge the template at the back of the book to the required size and trace the outlines with a transfer pencil. Follow the manufacturer's instructions to iron the design on to the calico.

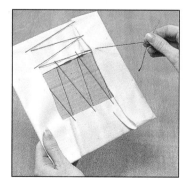

2 Stretch the calico in an embroidery hoop and work over the outlines using two strands of black embroidery thread in simple straight and satin stitches. Work legs and antennae in small chain stitch. Pick out a few details in colour. Press lightly from the wrong side when complete.

3 To mount the embroidery, place the card centrally on the back of the work and fold two opposite sides over it. Lace together with strong thread, then repeat with the other two sides. Write labels for the three orders of insects: Hymenoptera (bees and wasps), Lepidoptera (butterflies) and Coleoptera (beetles). Fix these to the fabric and insert it in the frame.

SPIDER BUTTONS

Brighten up a child's coat (or your own!) with these friendly spiders. Use the metal buttons that are sold for covering in fabric and match the size to your buttonholes. Snap the fronts on to the button backs before you start to decorate them. You can coat the baked buttons with a gloss varnish, if you wish.

YOU WILL NEED

MATERIALS
polymer clay: bright green, black and white
set of metal buttons
clear gloss varnish (optional)

EQUIPMENT
rolling pin
craft knife
cutting mat
paintbrush (optional)

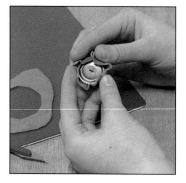

1 Roll the green clay out thinly and cut a circle large enough to cover the button. Mould the clay over the button.

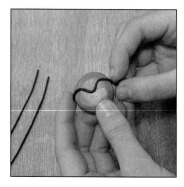

2 Using black clay, roll very thin strands for the legs and press them on to the button. Roll a finer strand for the spider's thread.

3 Roll a pea-sized ball of black clay and press it into the centre of the button for the spider's body.

4 Roll two small balls of white clay and press in position to make the eyes. Make the pupils from tiny black balls. Bake in a low oven following the manufacturer's instructions.

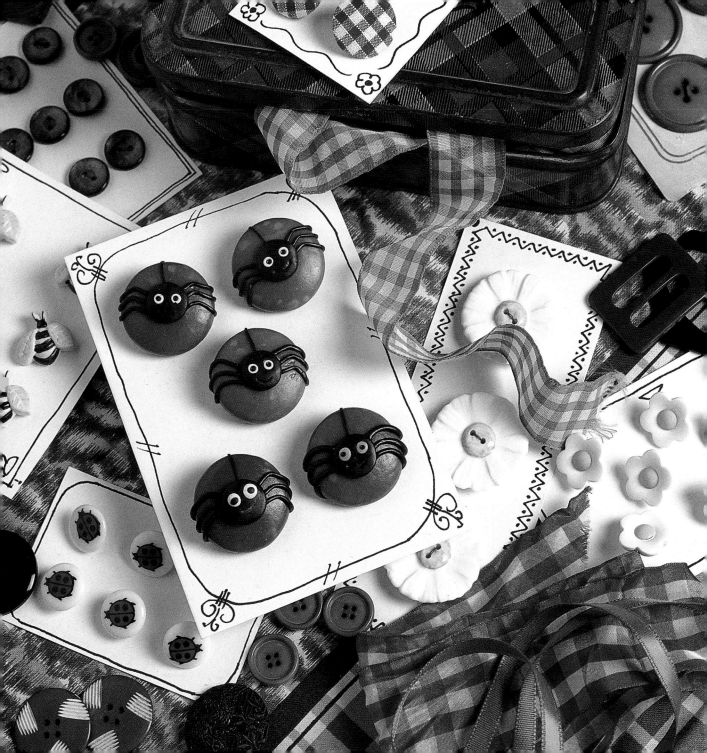

MOSAIC DRAGONFLY PLAQUE

Very effective mosaics can be made using broken china, fixing the pieces with ceramic adhesive and grouting just as you would when laying tiles. The old, chipped plates you were going to throw out may be just the colours you need.

YOU WILL NEED

MATERIALS
6 mm/¼ in sheet of birch
  plywood, 51 cm/20 in square
PVA glue
acrylic primer
dark green acrylic paint
electric cable
selection of china
tile adhesive
coloured tile grout

EQUIPMENT
fret saw or coping saw
bradawl
paintbrush
sandpaper
cable strippers
tile nippers
rubber gloves
nail brush
cloth

PREPARATION
Trace the template from the back of the book and enlarge. Transfer on to the plywood. Cut out the dragonfly and make two holes at the top of the body with a bradawl. Seal the front surface with diluted PVA glue and the back with acrylic primer. Leave to dry. Sand the back surface and paint with green acrylic paint.

1 Strip some electric cable and cut a short length of wire. Push this through the holes from the back and twist together securely.

2 Cut the china into regular shapes using tile nippers. Dip each piece into the tile adhesive, scooping up a thick layer, and press down securely. Leave to dry overnight.

3 Press the grout into the gaps between the china. Leave to dry for five minutes, then brush off the excess with a nail brush. Leave for another five minutes then polish with a cloth.

TEMPLATES

To enlarge the templates to the correct size, either use a grid system or a photocopier. For the grid system, trace the template and draw a grid of evenly spaced squares over your tracing. To scale up, draw a larger grid on to another piece of paper. Copy the outline on to the second grid by taking each square individually and drawing the relevant part of the outline in the larger square. For tracing templates you will need tracing paper, a pencil, card or paper, and scissors.

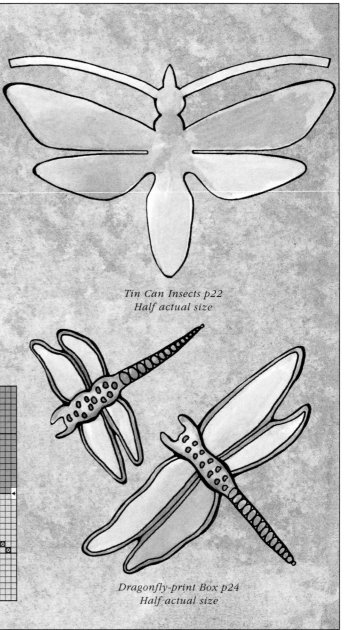

Tin Can Insects p22
Half actual size

Dragonfly-print Box p24
Half actual size

Needlepoint Beetle p19

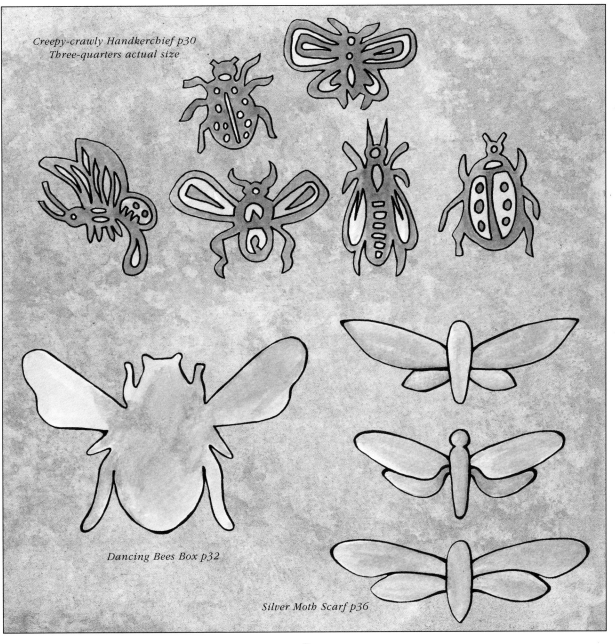

Creepy-crawly Handkerchief p30
Three-quarters actual size

Dancing Bees Box p32

Silver Moth Scarf p36

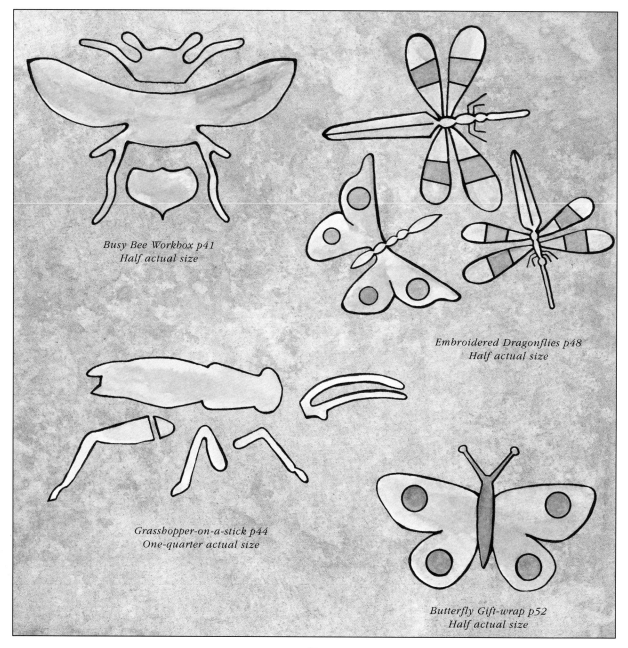

Busy Bee Workbox p41
Half actual size

Embroidered Dragonflies p48
Half actual size

Grasshopper-on-a-stick p44
One-quarter actual size

Butterfly Gift-wrap p52
Half actual size

Embroidered Insect Display p54
Half actual size

Mosaic Dragonfly Plaque p58
One-quarter actual size; half of
template shown

ACKNOWLEDGEMENTS

The publisher would like to thank the following people for designing the projects in this book.

Ofer Acoo
Spider's Web Brooch pp16–18;
Insect Storage Box pp38–40

Penny Boylan
Beetle Stationery pp12–13;
Needlepoint Beetle pp19–21

Louise Brownlow
Embroidered Dragonflies
pp48–51

Lucinda Ganderton
Creepy-crawly Handkerchief
pp30–31;
Embroidered Insect Display
pp54–55

Andrew Gilmore
Salt and Pepper Bugs pp26–29

David Hancock
Busy Bee Workbox pp41–43;
Grasshopper-on-a-stick pp44–45

Jill Hancock
Spider's Web Clock pp34–35

Mary Maguire
Spider Buttons pp56–57

Cleo Mussi
Mosaic Dragonfly Plaque
pp58–59

Deborah Schneebeli-Morrell
Tin can Insects pp22–23;
Sgraffito Egg pp46–47

Isabel Stanley
Silver Moth Scarf pp36–37

Emma Whitfield
Dragonfly-print Box pp24–25;
Dancing Bees Box pp32–33

Josephine Whitfield
Child's Ladybird Chair pp14–15;
Butterfly Gift-wrap pp52–53

Picture Credits
Pages 8–11: Christie's Images.